Tracing the Curve

Tracing the Curve

poems

Ariana Moulton

atmosphere press

For my family of writers, painters, musicians, teachers, carpenters, and athletes.

May the four winds blow you safely home.
-Jerry Garcia

Contents

8

1

Trace the Curve

for Lori Lightfoot

What if someone told you
you couldn't go where you normally go?
Would the *you* in you come undone?

Not seeing what you expect to see.
You're not alone in your quarantine,
except you are, globally masked, tightly tonight.

Would you even know if someone rearranged your desk at work,
moved your ruler aside, borrowed your protractor
and traced the curve we aim to flatten?

It's these flat lands where the wind sweeps for miles,
I see in my sleep, particles like dust.
Keeping us awake, watchmen of an invisible enemy.

If you've never been told no then how would you know
you wouldn't go back there, to that place you're supposed to be?
You would have grabbed more of your things, that ruler.

How could you measure freedoms of the past you've never lost?
Until this moment, when Madam Mayor quotes a poet,
Ms. Brooks herself, calling upon us to cultivate '*dreams in the dark*'.

It's bigger than us, microscopically and
'*it wants to crumble you down, to sicken you*'.
Your words bring us all, to a place where gold will attach itself

as we breathe freely tonight.

I'll Let You In

Drinking coffee black as iron,
the expectant teacher, still quarantined today.
My class dings digital doorbells,
this checkered screen,
ancillary attendance.

Ariel's corner square holds two.
A smirk, a smile, a younger face so dear.
Come near, who are you?
Your cousin leans into you,

to hear our daily schedule,
to see us sign the Pledge of Allegiance.
Her allegiance shown in her snuggle,
her need to connect, you protect.

I only hope I'm opaque enough in this moment
to block news feeds, fed with anger,
while Minneapolis screams for Floyd,
for innocent iron souls,
my role, to welcome, to protect our visitor.

A six-year-old whose Wi-Fi must have been down,
whose mother's essentially working.
Come in, I'll read to you of an imaginary
mouse who's searching for his lost love.

It's only love that can save us all
from concrete fractures,
a century of flames that have licked liberally
against you.

A Ballot or a Wing?

My mother's not afraid
of thrashing in the
woods, the dark noise
she can't see on her
morning run.

Her September breath
is company enough,
steam melts a fear
that isn't there.

She is this morning's
watchman hoping to
lock eyes with a Barred
Owl.

Black and white night,
deceptive branches.
She told me she's afraid
of this election, so visible.

No tree limbs in her way,
a flashing screen
tells of lit lies from a
leader we didn't elect.

She fears a forest of facts
that crackle, that snap.
Was that a ballot or a wing
that swooped her up?

Took her to places
where only the mind
can go, where maybe a
Justice who passed could
save us.

Her black gown
of feathers a wingspan,
If only it could span the living,
those fearing what we see.

The Black Bear on the 11th Hole

I forgot to write the poem
about facing the bear.
When June was still rising
and the Vermont woods
bore low hanging fruit.
People around town
said bears were lumbering
down from the mountains,
finding sitting duck bird feeders,
a loose lid on the garbage tin.
We ran the graveled path
around the golf course,
a friend and I. Our gates
not the same. I faked
I could keep up.
Our banter bounced
off the pines, kicking the pebbles,
with our overpriced sneakers.
I looked a few steps ahead,
under my blue brim.
We trudged the last hill
near the 11th hole, I'm told.
She grabbed my hip, that grip,
I felt her silent fear.
"We have to turn around,"
she said. The bear's head,
a mascot costume, a body,
smaller than imagined.
Aren't our fears
always this way? Smaller
than we imagined.
When we face them,
breathless, beyond

ourselves.
Whatever's on your shelf,
a distorted shadow,
a figure in the dark,
may need dusting.
Beware the unattended
items lurking inside folds.
For they too need
dew covered fruit amongst
the pines. Uncover and
face the poem
you forgot to write.

For the Man Under the Viaduct at Barry

When I see the man
who appeared in my poem
it feels like a mistake.
His place is only in print,
between pages 63 and 65.
I thought I had
captured him,
kept him.
He would stay there.
A metaphor,
an image.
He doesn't know his
cracked feet found their way
into my book.
Or that his glasses
let him see
past the stars.
Now he peers
at a glowing screen,
still near the lake, in the dark.
Where he could read what I wrote
about him, of his
curved imprinted back,
arched like the bridge.
Neither of us
stay where we are.
When Zeus placed Cancer,
the crab, in the Y-shaped sky,
He knew he'd end up
in a book of myths,
God-like,
not forgotten
on a bench.

Permanence plays
no favorites amongst
this morning's cobwebs
I've jogged through,
their draglines like
connected stars,
like tightropes you've
never balanced on.

Waiting for Tuesday

When you've had a molar pulled
and the house is out of Advil,
your tongue twists around
the root still in your gums.

Early alley workers can't see
into the crimping canal.
Their paver hums louder
than yesterday's sirens,
Saturday's ignited dumpsters.

This City of Broad Shoulders
knows the Great Fire ended
when God sent a rainstorm,
citizens looked to the Chicago sky.
Ash covered cheeks.

Today's fatigue, no shovel too heavy
for Chicago to lift,
when glass speckles our streets,
needing to be thrown back to heaven.

A Chicagoan would know it was
Kerfoot's sign that read,
"All gone, except my wife, my children,
and my energy."
His grit, his only ibuprofen.

We Are The Storm

Most of the women I know
are too nice, too organized
for their own good,
too calendar savvy.
Can plan a week
for a family of five with
a few clicks, while staying
fit, while volunteering,
and baking gluten free
muffins from scratch.
You can't match their
ability to smile through
bitter eyes, their disguise
is their tight waist, their 401k
their 8 minute mile.
But where does the branch
detach from, when a dish
drops onto tile and
the mascara runs?
Beware lady lions
who have left your dens.
It's the jungle that should
be warned for we are the storm,
the anxiety driven doers
who make appointments
in the dark, work meetings
from the park and make
it all look too easy.

Make it all look, too easy.

Suppose God Joined In

She always knew
        she was a hero.

Played hospital in uniform,
        red cross
        across her forehead,

    pretending germs
        were real.

She knew
  which band-aid to choose,
    to mend
      a stuffed animal's wound,
to keep the pain from spreading.

Her palms marked
        all she touched,
            brushed,
dispersing the invisible.

Today she knows
        she's the soldier
            in scrubs,
    as she heads toward the train,
        deployed into an empty car.

Is she wondering where
        she left her mask,
            her toy stethoscope,
                and what she would ask of God,

if He joined her?
        .

The Answer's in Belmont Harbor

Is there a word for when
the Lake swallows
a teenager on Monday,
just before dinner?

Was it four friends or teammates,
who jumped in?

Who wouldn't want to feel
a strength greater than their own
just for a moment?

Forget what teasing sounds like,
have water weigh you under.

Could the lake show its
violent mouth, defeated limbs,
white noise?

How many mothers
mouthed the words,
"Thank God,"when the evening news echoed,
the rescue turned recovery?

Was their son dry, at home with them?
When four became three,
accident slipped from our vocabulary.

Where was the wordless boy when crashing
ripped him from a place
where his hand could grip a rung,
a teammate's slipping fingers?

Will it be his body that tells the survivors
what to say when the moonlight
finds him?

A Sister Knows

My mother is the eldest of five.
        Cork, Ireland.
                She lies in the dark,

a solar powered strand of lights
        telling her it's still night.
        Reminding her that
                yesterday's sun was strong enough,

that strawberry cheeks
        are asleep across her old farmhouse,
                across floorboards that creak,

behind doors that stick in the humidity.
        Her feet, bare and silent
                whisper her namesake,

Wendy, as if she's
        in the nursery tonight,
                John & Micheal twin bedded
                and Nana at their side.

It's Wendy, we know
        whose nightgown
        floats with an ease,
                so others can rest.

While Tinkerbell's lights
        may guide her to a place
        where she doesn't have
                to take care of anybody.

In Neverland, the stars are in charge
        and birth order is reversed,
                while pirates swirl backwards

into the night,
  the ocean freeway.
  Because 'never is an awfully long time'
    and it's 'on the wind's back'
you can go.

April's Not Awake

The virus seeps
into my dream.
A car.
A laughing dog
walker
calls it
"the 'rona."
No one washes
their hands
upside down,
speeds in reverse.
Time rises
temperatures,
REM cycles,
warn commuters
of smog
delays.
Distress in
delight.
When April's
not awake
enough to
call me names.

Between a Breathing Machine and My Screen

What must you think of our cartoon explanation,
the map of your home country covered in human silhouettes,
connected, dot to dot in red lines?

You stood at your desk, intent on understanding
our attempt to understand how a virus becomes a lesson plan,
an unplanned action plan in this classroom.

Is there room for these characters to lay,
one next to the other, in beds uncounted, recounted.
Where would we make a breathing machine if not in your country?

If I was 8, it might have been a record playing
"We Are the World" that had me listening to grooves as they
spun under the needle, no vaccine can drip through.

Your mother didn't tell you what corner of the world would
become your new world or how you would absorb our characters
so quickly.

I see the flames in your eyes,
that whimsical horse you draw
as if your hand can cut and paste its spirit.

But how clearly you understood when I said,
"Fire is the poor man's friend,'"
with a spark you said, "He can steal!"

My, how you're right, not left behind
finding that screen deceiving, xenophobic
and wrong.

Mistaken As

Of course you and he are sleeping
under the viaduct,
where it's typically dry,
hidden from weather.
I don't blame you,
huddled and folded together,
a fetal position.
You're still,
waiting for nothing.
A sign erected,
a surrender.
Not to be mistaken as
a brush pile,
or forgotten laundry.
The occasional early morning runner
silently gasps, side stepping your bed,
a cardboard box spring.
But today I know
that the protection you seek
is not of your marriage,
but simply of each other.
Two young men,
embraced below a street,
which itself never sleeps.

2

String of Pearls

The stars must have been out last night,
because I found Orion's belt laying in the dew,
the Seven Sisters disappearing into dawn.

When blades glisten with bulbs of moisture
and constellations converse on the lawn,
my mind drifts westward, thoughts clinging to a shooting star.

How far could the Big Dipper take me?
To the shores of my lake, to Chicago's
re-opened bike path?

If the Milky Way spit me out on the corner
of Fletcher and Sheffield,
could dew drops paint protest signs?

Could stardust send messages of
impartiality, echos of fear,
this near to my apartment?

Would spotting the eponymous
hunter protect me from
an arrow made of stars?

But in this moment, this valley's asleep
and it's only the distant bullfrog that
can catch a string of pearls.

Vermeer's Girl

When I was young,
she wasn't shadowed so gorgeously
turned and profiled in light he was known for.
A glimmering earring.
Perhaps that dusty blue
was an afterthought that day.
A turban so twisted.
Imagine the strength of the hands
that would bind you, cause you to look.
The whites of your eyes,
the fear, that blue arching forehead,
knowing you'll never age in our eyes,
we're stunned by your lines.
No word for beauty or aged paint.
When Vermeer hovered his brush,
crinkling your coppered coat,
catching our breath,
for so long.

No Painting Should Match Your Couch

for Josh, the Hall of Famer

It's not the unpainted canvas that draws him near,
the brilliant buoys of Maine that hang like earrings on a net,
their oranges brighter than a hue he can mix.

It's not a painting that will match your couch, or carpet,
but a stolen glance into a soul selling papers solely to you.
You won't notice the barbed wire that's diagonal across such
beauty, it's sharp subtlety splicing the clay roofs of a Croatian cliff.

Never doubt that his eyes are like cameras,
housing their own darkroom, their own memory card,
a vault of hues never imagined and scenes unseen.

We can't see what happens when an artist leaves room for the
     unimaginable.
We are simply honored onlookers, looking for a familiar flower or
detailed tower, whose floor we may have once lived on.

With legacy living on and design in his DNA,
it only makes sense for the blank canvas
to be a stage silently set for the dance of his brush.

The Nearness of Wasps

I can't tell if I remember being four.
A dirt road day on Spring Turn,
the name my father gave to our corner
where trucks speed,
cloud puffs, dry mouth.

I can't say if the memory is mine,
folded under Summer's buzz.
Pictures tell me what to know,
what to remember when thinking back
on rural days.

I can't feel my brother's hand
in mine, 20 months wiser.
Sticky summer palms,
strawberry cheeks too red,
too rosy.

The bees on invisible strings,
flew rings around our
blonder hair, the nearness of wasps,
a dancing willow.

Bend low the branches,
hair swinging, canopied
tree castle, arrow shaped leaves
in August say nothing of fall.

We knew Beaver Brook
beyond the sledding hill,
a singing stream,
paper boat swallowing
chorused babble.

Nothing at stake when
cut hay rolls into curved
climbing bales, scratched
thighs, fatigue.

Summer stung me then,
more alert the hum
of missing brother,
his hands in the dust.

Time, Divided

I hadn't been told that I would
spend so much of my time divided,
split between myself, a falsehood.

Amongst the thickest fog I have stood,
within liquid layers I've confided,
I hadn't been told that I would.

Draw peonies in a yard of pinkish girlhood,
back when hemispheres seemed so united.
Split between myself, a falsehood.

Another plunge in all likelihood,
morning synapses bloom, delighted.
I hadn't been told that I would.

When solutions arise and aren't for good,
dreams burn deep, ignited.
Split between myself, a falsehood.

There's not a map to womanhood.
Has my path been blighted?
I hadn't been told that I would,
split between myself, a falsehood.

Where Would Children Go?

I'm making a list,
a T-chart,
to divide the permanent changes
from the temporary changes.

I know the sun will rise
where Lake Michigan
licks the horizon,
revealing hues of orange.
Tulips will reappear in spring
like holiday bulbs.

But are we destined to be
better hand washers,
elbow bump forever
and work from home?

Where would the children go
to sing together
a song about posies,
a tissue, a tissue,
we all fall down?

When laptops become
classrooms and
dirt is pushed aside
it's only this morning's breath
that draws the line.

Leaving Spring Turn

Because saying goodbye
feels like hot twisting in my
chest, breathless and bent over.
Because not knowing when I'll
see my parents again isn't
what I had planned.
I don't wonder if I could
use all my fire, my
many wishes to singe
out the virus, beat it down
to dust, to ashes.
It's only the variety of song birds
this July morning, holding
me back, drying my eyes.
I saw the upside down bird
last night, his head like a weight,
an involuntary downswing.
But aren't we all caught in the
upside down, when a droplet
shatters into pieces, releases
expectations and spirals into
a single bird?
To unpack and repack
stirs up feathers.
The truth being--
that not knowing
is enough.

Why I Can't Exhale

Love in the time of distancing
proves to be tough.

Are you more than six feet apart
tonight in your king-sized bed?

Or could love take you to a galaxy
where a microscope reveals crowned planets?

Corona cones float,
a weightless wait of wonder.

The pock marked map,
your eyelids, like screens
dots bleeding beyond borders.

Seep through lying leaders
who name call and, you might recall
floating planets hover outside your bloodstream.

We used to memorize our lover's face,
their breaths a reminder.
You could be crowned, one day.

But who would look closely enough,
while distancing, to see how royal
we are?

Seeing Through Vaulted Sheets

When you're 9
and it's the eve
of your birthday,
you build a fort with
your sister.
Pink sheets,
vaulted ceilings,
toy trunks, foundations,
and pillars.
The tacked up
fabric drapes,
so you can see
no further
than a day
into the future.
The day of your birth,
did Aries know you
were breach,
a heads up
we all waited for?
Tonight I see the
tents in Central Park
hastily staked,
assembled where
Manhattan assembles,
a priceless view.
You viewed too tightly
as the white boats,
like counties,
steamed through
the Hudson.
How could you wait
for 10 tonight?

When the doctor found
you turned the wrong way,
feathers danced themselves
into the shape
of the Ram, his stars,
not candles,
to be blown out
just once.

Have You Sanitized?

Don't we have to be our own answer today,
when the sun glazes the oak outside my window?
Not solving the mystery of the hawk I saw,
no lingering nest to write about.

The dove in his morning place.
Nothing these days has staying power.
Even our screens vanish into dust.
Reports tell me Nairobi braces itself.

The wealthy wear designer masks.
This luxury won't reach nearby Kibera.
Tin roofs too warm, too crowded,
this infected April.

A boy sings,
"Have you sanitized?"
His lyrics don't have
a word for quarantine.

I mean, where would you look,
if not inside yourself,
to choose which solution
to be part of?

Below the Peak

In New Hampshire,
the seniors rode up a ski lift to graduate,
no skis or heavy boots to swing.

Each chair hung safely distanced,
far enough for gowns to dance above
naked trails.

I imagine a crackled Pomp and Circumstance
called from the lodge,
moving them to set victory.

To wait their turn,
extend an eager hand,
disinfected diplomas.

I've never walked off
a chairlift so lifted with
accomplished breeze.

Did they throw their hats
into a flock of ravens that day,
a furried flutter?

Time must have come for them to descend,
to choose a trail, black diamond,
blue circle.

It's not easy to remember one
ride up the mountain
when your eyes are flooded with change

and tassels tell the story,
unwritten, your future
below the peak.

No Ticker Tape, No Parade

What joyful release will you imagine?
It won't be ticker tape
like confetti fluttering,
falling on Manhattan streets.
Or collective joy,
the defeat of Nazi Germany,
necks craning over balconies,
flags flying like bright kisses.
It might be watching leaves
that never fell in Winter
cling like a chrysalis in morning light,
too red for May.
In our own way
this passage of breath,
these deaths, a fallen leaf out of season
lands louder than stone on stone today.
It's not the crashed markets I hear
or newsreels reeling,
this feeling stays with the
morning "L" train.
Still on time, not empty
or distant enough to extinguish
our flaming hearts, our lungs.
No shared wonder can ignite
these muted days,
digitally boxed displays,
the pixilated joy
too painful in its attempt
to heal.

Remind Me Not to Let Myself Forget

I forget about the virus and its grip,
its crimson crowns like uninvited
mushrooms.

It's brief, this relief
from a mind braided with wonder,
with worry.

No hurry today to see infected
dust blow across the valley,
flutter on rounded bales.

To inhale this moment
means midnight stars
invade your lungs.

Your fears are no more
real than dreams.

Nothing grips
the bullfrog who's louder
than CNN tonight.

He catches your ear enough
to erase headlines,
to mute your radio's rhetoric.

3

Taken Back

for Chris Matthews, who left MSNBC

Was it hardball you wanted to play in the make-up room,
making up charmed remarks, placing orders,
in order to express what you didn't know would later
resurface as a truth, just hers?

What was hard about saying nothing, letting a beauty
be unnoticed, left alone to be? Just behave, just walk by.
The way you were taught, or not. You ought not comment
in these bulbed mirrors, amongst crimson lipsticks.

Stick with *The Examiner, The Chronicle, The Times,*
have changed us, catch up, catch that hardball, bare handed.
Grip this me too, this me three, this me we. The lid has popped off.
We're leaning in, meeting you at the microphone, watch your tone.

Let's play hardball! A gruff order, ordered out daily.
Now let us tell you what we really think.
It's that hand on our lower back, the lengthened squeeze,
a glance at our knees.

Consider the night taken back.

Dear Mom,

I heard a man say
the game had been figured out
hijacked, hacked of hope
circumvented with clicks,
tricks of trade that will no doubt invade.
I heard another man say
it was true that top dogs
found weak blogs,
weak markets,
and weaker minds to trick,
to add smoke to mirrors,
but nothing's clearer to me,
rules are made to protect
inventors of the game.
Had founding fathers
been founding mothers
colleges would never be electoral.
True votes collected counted,
mounted for the public to breathe in,
and out would go the age of cheating,
hiding the old maid under the rug
blindfolding one's opponent
past the point of power.
When Nike stood in Athena's
outstretched hand,
her laurel wreath around her neck,
she knew it was her who would keep her wings,
not to be shed.
With those wings came flight,
reins tightly gripped, not slipped,
no slight of hand, to misunderstand between souls.
A conversation, a round table
topped with lost languages

only spoken out of truth,
commitment, no equipment needed.
A single chariot stampede,
wings spread may be the light
that's missing, this country's Vitamin D.
And Mom, to you who kept
your name, your laurel crown,
I say, we take these reins.

Pirouetting to the Dishwasher

Because I was taught
that boredom sets only
in a boring mind,
I'm keeping my mouth shut,
locked with a small key.
A jewelry box,
a spinning ballerina, stuck.
I've spiraled into a place
where unloading the
dishwasher feels like
a competitive sport.
My toes, in a permanent
pirouette may drill through
the floor. Staying in one
place, a cyclone.
At least I could
peer into the apartment below?
Throw a rope down,
lower myself in my tutu.
Do they have better snacks
or a piano for plunking?
Would they wonder how
I came to be dressed like
a tiny dancer, while I
rummage through cabinets
of gourmet crackers?
Even a crack in the wall
would catch my eye,
mid-twirl, satin ribbons
pulling me through,
to any place without
strings, without a song

that repeats when it's
wound.

Tell the Cacti

If you were told it would
be a year before you would
return to your normal life,
what would you do before
it all folded in?

Would you and your spouse
find the freshest Farmer's Market
and wander the earthy crowd for overpriced
berries, the cherries coupled
together?

Would you follow a cloud of dust
towards a desert you've never seen
and tell the cacti to hold
tight to each droplet,
for change is coming?

Would you take in a show,
with an audience of lovers,
touch shoulders with a stranger
in the eleventh row, let limbs
linger on the armrest?

None of us cancel a year,
or wish for for the planet
to fold, I was told two weeks
before cheeks fevered
cherry red, dusted with
questions.

Wedding at Belmont Harbor

A wedding today,
no broom,
to jump over,
to sweep storm debris.
The procession curved
the sandy path
at Belmont Harbor.
Her tight lace dress,
short enough for walking.
A Covid wedding,
no pews, no falling rice.
Like hail from Monday's storm,
the funnel cloud,
not whirling her train
into the sky.
A grandmother
looks down,
her audience of one.
The photographer,
draped in straps,
follows them
to side streets.
No important places,
no ballroom, no caught
bouquet. No rice.
No parting gift
on her terms.
So much
to let go of.

Don't Ask Me That

I pinch my 10-year-old's leg,
as she licks her cone,
the summer's ending.

If it was all a dream,
I tell her, she wouldn't feel my
fingers, my grown out
manicure, my nails.

We don't charge
our phones,
eat reheated pizza
in a dream, honey.

What a long slumber
it would be.
She references March,
the St. Patty's Day
we all stayed in.

Our unlucky noses
pressed shamrocks on the glass.
We searched for life
in the streets,
A neighbor breaking the rules.

How do you reassure
yourself, your child,
that dreams are saved
for the obscure?

The cones that never end,
never drip in August's lull.

I could explain that
her purple bike would
never fall outside,
over there, behind her
closed eyes.

But skinned knees
know the truth,
that mothers
are awake
this questioning
evening.

My Teaching is Only as Good as My Wi-Fi

My 7 year old won't eat her lunch
in a loud cafeteria.
Won't unzip a new lunch bag
to find a note from me.
Her sister won't look for her
locker amongst her deodorant-
scented friends,
a combination of nerves.
The bell rings for no one
on the front steps of their building--
bricks set in 1871.
Where The Fire's survivors
once gathered.
No spark of a virus.
The power's already
flickering today,
no back-up plan
to say where
the breaker is.
Where their friends are,
their checkered classmates.
Their veteran teacher
glitches when the
Wi-Fi goes out.

The Prayer of Nikki Giovanni

After "Rosa Parks," Nikki Giovanni

This is for the teachers who left in a furry gathering
what they could, leaving schedules unerased,
a trail of papers to crumble, to flutter like ash.

This is for the conductor alone in his silver "L" train
each car voiceless and vulnerable. A single passenger passing
between cars, no paid Ventra card, no final stop.

This is for the man that I see near the lake, his grey
sleeping bag staked like a tent, his weathered fingers
roll a cigarette, smudged glasses, CNN not ringing in his ears.

This is for the woman in scrubs I saw, cigarette to her lips.
We grip what we can, what we can, when a climate clamps
down on our lungs.

This is for that teenager on my block I watched,
his hands behind his back, his backpack taken from
him. The police, six of them.

This is for the boy in my daughter's class whose blood
filled with cancer, his tired body, resilient like metal.

This is for the graduate, the new hire, whose first day
was September 11th, 2001. His train was running late
to tunnel him to Manhattan.

This is for my mail carrier, Oliver who honks
when he arrives, waves at my daughters.

May his trusted hands, that canvas bag, carry my ballot
over this great lake, to be counted at all costs
in a time when we all know what this is for.

Tinsel

You didn't know that there was a part of you
that still wanted to believe, to be convinced.
But when 2 am finds you and the front steps glisten,
you can't help but turn your head in wonder.

Wondering which direction those lights came from,
suddenly streaked and silent.
Tonight's streets hold an absence that's intangible,
a balmy fog, unseasonably warm.

If it weren't for my age,
I would have sworn I heard bells,
beyond the L-Train,
beneath that part of me that must have stopped believing.

I believe tonight is different, as I walk our 4 month old puppy,
us both in a slumber.
We can sense the city is braced, ready to be graced.
I never know what it is that turns our dog's head,

a scurrying city critter, or a suspicious figure dashing away.
But I know I once dreamed his nose was red, and he was the
sleigh's hero, afloat above Fletcher Street.
But isn't that the best part of believing?

You're beyond the logic of streets, passed the sum of the parts,
where the unimaginable is imagined.
I imagine my daughters will wake soon,
quietly slumber down carpeted stairs--pausing to decide what is real.

I only hope they'll notice the intentional cookie crumbs left
believably, just for them.

Worship

The smell of cut grass
reminds me of my father.
His riding mower a church pew,
a daily prayer.
This field his bible verse,
as he avoids Box Elders,
rooted steeples.
The mower's hum,
a faint puff of diesel.
Neighbors pass lanes of green
drawn on our bumpy single acre.
Given the chance,
he would mow in heaven,
landscaping the afterlife,
his wife trimming
the pine's lowest branches,
removing sticks,
a firmament of pinecones.
A call to worship,
his John Deere
carriaging him off
for miles.

Consider the Tulip

mercury's migration
this morning's thermometer
petals puckered
closed cold in coral
emerald stems bend east
floral yoga

The Battle at Abernathy Place

My mother doesn't run with her legs.
Toned in tones of caramel, petite and strong.

It's her heart that plows up a gravel hill,
one well-fit sneaker in front of the other.

What resolve must a mother search for,
her daily "Om," on hills that crest just out of reach.

Not to lessen her simple jog,
a morning fog lifting beyond a dew covered field

that yields the occasional wild turkey, dark and fat.
She may not peek up from her hat to see,

mountains that lay like elephants,
trunks extended out, a reach.

It's not a stretch to say she replays work meetings in her head,
predicts future arguments.

It's tense, this drive, deep breaths not deep enough,
an exhale could impale.

But the road forks in time to let
thorns retract while drops of sweat
crash lightly.

If God Took Away Your Cell Phone

If God took away your cell phone,
your remaining landline and your Wi-Fi,
You might remember where you put that pen,
that pad of paper you used to keep by your bed.

The one that held ideas, sketches,
a love letter to your wife.
Dusting it off might mean leaving a note,
"Went to the store, be back in a bit."

Was it so bad when we walked to the neighbor's
to borrow a cup of milk or today's paper?
Today's paper might be blank, presses stopped,
worker's hands free of ink, no type to set.

The invisible headline not saying what we know.
Don't drive to the unnecessary, you don't have to.
Do you need to have a globe under your hands,
that glowing screen to swipe?

I imagine God might text Mary,
to remind her they're out of milk,
the cow is sick, no act can cure.
Would she ghost him, leaving him to wonder

where she left her pen?

Your Will to Greet

to a young Emily Dickinson

I wasn't sure it was possible
to think I was you,
or write in the voice of another.
I could speak as a sea captain
from a painting's tempest.
Steal words from an aging artist
painting from above the ocean,
looking down or looking nowhere
but into his canvas.

I wasn't sure if taking your voice
would be polite or understood.
For clearly you weren't.
The forced edits pressed upon you,
lengthening your slanting lines
to appease known poets.
Not knowing you gives me courage
to dream our labyrinths link,
our reclusiveness resonates through time.

I wasn't sure why you left school like I did.
Why a homeward retreat would be needed, suggested.
Your furrowed brow, your
'Noted penchant for white clothing'
don't frighten me.

What reluctance took over,
took away your will to greet others,
to leave your saving bedroom,
your dangerous pen?
What scratched you so deeply
you never married,
only kept friends through

quilled correspondence?

Since you're not able to explain yourself,
not that you would anyway,
I'm left with lingering thoughts,
there was an unquiet mind
too great for greetings,
too frenzied for friendships
that might bore such brilliance.

Overall, speaking to you is quite easy.
Your affinity towards death drove
that door more firmly closed.
Your sabbath at home,
not a place of worship,
in the tempest
of your swelling ocean.

Take Two

For Anne Sexton Who Was Prescribed Poetry

And call me in the morning.
5 mg of metaphor and 1,200 of iambic pentameter.
Take with food, write each accelerated heartbeat
into a rhythm that counts countless capsules.

Take two children, combine noble thoughts,
an unquiet mind, a political playscape
escaping the country's grasp,
childproof the lid and call it confessional poetry.

Storytellers veil the story until it's written,
you wrote in '59, but at 45, your last chapter
punctuated by your own hand, you feared
you were closer to fine, creativity spiraling,
draining the already drained.

What would you say to your daughters
who dutifully downed the spoonful,
without question, without their mother?
The early spokeswoman for poetry prescribed.

Children of ice,
praying to the morbidly still,
your words dosed high enough,
to deliver you to the crying moon.

Mother

Are you sure we're not part Menomonee?
Because I see myself better in the dark,
black feathers find me
while the moon wavers on inlet water.

Mother, they've carved you into metal,
full headdress, mounted on your unnamed horse.
My steps too loud on this Illinois dust,
they disrupt.

I think I should float above the land,
a whisper passing like willow branches,
like peaceful smoke,
I choke on love for you this morning,

I could cast a line from this crest,
a spider's thread and walk across it.
Pray your metal hand would reach out.

No doubt, today ages us all.
You told me, it's up to us
to see patterns in fog
that have come before us,
have made us.

When You're Whole

My therapist's grandmother
taught her, "you eat last."
The woman, the cook,
barefoot in the kitchen.
You serve them, those men,
each child.
You eat last.
We don't hear our
stomachs' moan,
women's work crashes
between our ears,
years upon years.
You eat last.
Our hands know
layers of wives
never found solace,
an apron knotted
tighter, knuckles
like wood.
You eat last.
Are we shadows,
moving without sound?
A knife rapidly chops
a rhythm, a window
a beat.
You eat last.
You eat last.
You eat last.
Or come down,
come out of the dawn
you awoke in.
No shadow surrounds
you when you're

whole. It's power you find
when you've been last,
when you've been last.
Beware the right hand pass,
the right hand pass.
Silent acceleration,
a nation braced with
an election, a beam,
a vice presidential candidate
of colors now seen,
colors now seen.

Ask the Leaves

Even the reddest leaves
tell me their anxiety,
fevered, nature's ink.

My inkling to pocket each one,
save them, jar their cells,
hues I want to live with.

I can't imagine a place
without an October,
crisp and sober.

My chapped lips
tell me it's vest weather,
do I dare to turn the heat on,
or grab a sweater?

An 8 year old tells me
he raked his
neighbor's leaves,
growing his pile,
that snapping igloo of orange.

I can't tell what is a leaf
or a ballot, paper fingering,
leafing through, the who,
the who nots.

The scared leaf
left on its branch
too long, hangs on.

Knocking on November's
door, saving itself for
voting day.

It may flutter down
and slip itself into a ballot box,
metal and locked.

No Line Breaks

My father taught poetry
writing to prisoners
at the Great Meadow
Correctional Facility.
Words belong to us all,
he didn't need to say.
I don't know how many
clearance forms he filled out,
how many times they took
his fingerprints,
those soft poet hands
don't remember
I visited David, my
friend's brother.
Cook County Correctional
Center, a federal prison.
Alliteration altered my vision
bulletproof plexiglass.
He wanted to hear of the outside,
the over there of summer.
What did Lake Michigan feel
like on free bare feet?
He didn't know of my poet
Dad or how to rewrite the
night he stood on the wrong
corner, picked up by a friend
who didn't murder anyone.
No line breaks in his line up,
no metaphor for handcuffed
hands whose innocent
prints needed a pen, a slip of
paper to slip between bars.

Notes to Dad, in Regards to Your Books

1.
I got your letter today.
I read it four times.
In reference to your
request, I have a few questions.
How many books?

2.
Too many to count?
And there are more in the cabin?
Original copies with signatures,
crinkled bent pages,
a black and white polaroid between
page four and five.

3.
This could take years,
bury me literally
under Yeats, Frost and Oliver.
Am I up to the task? You asked.

4.
Remember when you wrote
of a fear? Of being at the pearly
gates with nothing to read.
I assure you.

5.
Yes, I recall your trip to
Powell's and Strand.
The night you dreamt
of Buenos Aires,
the bookshop capital of the world.

6.
When can I start?
First, build me a staircase
out of books you have two of.
*Moby Dick, Roots, Between a Rock
and a Hard Place.*
I'll book a flight.

7.
Second thoughts?
You're not sure you're
ready to get rid of any?
Books could become pillows
for those without beds
or morph into crinkled dollars.
Let's push through.

8.
Called mom today.
She said she can't find
you.

9.
Behind which stack?
Inside the chapter
where Gregor's stuck?
Move towards the sound of
Mom's voice.
Please.

10.
Your last letter
tells of winter coming,
those miles to go.

11.
I'm happy to hear
the wood stoves are
on. What if you run
out of newspaper
to crinkle into the ash?

12.
Yes it was a joke.
Burning books?
Surely you jest.
We could build
a path out of them,
like stones, lay them
in a pattern between
the house and the barn.
Mom can mulch between
Wordsworth and Plath.

13.
Cancel the flight?
You don't need assistance.
I'll hover above your study
on a floating page.
Just in case.

14.
Yours Truly.
Bound.

About Atmosphere Press

Atmosphere Press is an independent, full-service publisher for excellent books in all genres and for all audiences. Learn more about what we do at atmospherepress.com.

We encourage you to check out some of Atmosphere's latest releases, which are available at Amazon.com and via order from your local bookstore:

About the Author

Ariana Moulton is a 3rd grade teacher and writer living in Chicago with her two daughters and husband. She grew up in Cornwall, Vermont, attended Bates College and has her master's from Columbia College. She is inspired by nature, politics, Chicago, and the people and landscapes of Vermont. Her writing appears in *Verity LA*, *Poet's Choice*, *Lucky Jefferson*, *Poem Village*, and *What Rough Beast Covid 19 Edition*. *Tracing the Curve* is her first collection.